SONGS OF KABIR

LECTOR HOUSE PUBLIC DOMAIN WORKS

SONGS OF KABIR

KABIR,
RABINDRANATH TAGORE,
EVELYN UNDERHILL

9 789389 956924

ISBN: 978-93-89956-92-4

Published: 1915

LECTOR HOUSE

LECTOR HOUSE LLP
E-MAIL: lectorpublishing@gmail.com

SONGS OF KABÎR

BY

KABIR

TRANSLATED BY
RABINDRANATH TAGORE

AUTHOR OF "GITANJALI," ETC.

WITH THE ASSISTANCE OF
EVELYN UNDERHILL

1915

INTRODUCTION

I

The poet Kabîr, a selection from whose songs is here for the first time offered to English readers, is one of the most interesting personalities in the history of Indian mysticism. Born in or near Benares, of Mohammedan parents, and probably about the year 1440, he became in early life a disciple of the celebrated Hindu ascetic Râmânanda. Râmânanda had brought to Northern India the religious revival which Râmânuja, the great twelfth-century reformer of Brâhmanism, had initiated in the South. This revival was in part a reaction against the increasing formalism of the orthodox cult, in part an assertion of the demands of the heart as against the intense intellectualism of the Vedânta philosophy, the exaggerated monism which that philosophy proclaimed. It took in Râmânuja's preaching the form of an ardent personal devotion to the God Vishnu, as representing the personal aspect of the Divine Nature: that mystical "religion of love" which everywhere makes its appearance at a certain level of spiritual culture, and which creeds and philosophies are powerless to kill.

Though such a devotion is indigenous in Hinduism, and finds expression in many passages of the Bhagavad Gîtâ, there was in its mediæval revival a large element of syncretism. Râmânanda, through whom its spirit is said to have reached Kabîr, appears to have been a man of wide religious culture, and full of missionary enthusiasm. Living at the moment in which the impassioned poetry and deep philosophy of the great Persian mystics, Attâr, Sâdî, Jalâlu'ddîn Rûmî, and Hâfiz, were exercising a powerful influence on the religious thought of India, he dreamed of reconciling this intense and personal Mohammedan mysticism with the traditional theology of Brâhmanism. Some have regarded both these great religious leaders as influenced also by Christian thought and life: but as this is a point upon which competent authorities hold widely divergent views, its discussion is not attempted here. We may safely assert, however, that in their teachings, two—perhaps three—apparently antagonistic streams of intense spiritual culture met, as Jewish and Hellenistic thought met in the early Christian Church: and it is one of the outstanding characteristics of Kabîr's genius that he was able in his poems to fuse them into one.

A great religious reformer, the founder of a sect to which nearly a million northern Hindus still belong, it is yet supremely as a mystical poet that Kabîr lives for us. His fate has been that of many revealers of Reality. A hater of religious exclusivism, and seeking above all things to initiate men into the liberty of the children of God, his followers have honoured his memory by re-erecting in a new place the barriers which he laboured to cast down. But his wonderful songs survive, the spontaneous expressions of his vision and his love; and it is by these, not by the didactic teachings associated with his name, that he makes his immortal appeal to the heart. In these poems a wide range of mystical emotion is brought into play: from the loftiest abstractions, the most otherworldly passion for the Infinite, to the most intimate and personal realization of God, expressed in homely metaphors and religious symbols drawn indifferently from Hindu and Mohammedan belief. It is impossible to say of their author that he was Brâhman or Sûfî, Vedântist or Vaishnavite. He is, as he says himself, "at once the child of Allah and of Râm." That Supreme Spirit Whom he knew and adored, and to Whose joyous friendship he sought to induct the souls of other men, transcended whilst He included all metaphysical categories, all credal definitions; yet each contributed something to the description of that Infinite and Simple Totality Who revealed Himself, according to their measure, to the faithful lovers of all creeds.

Kabîr's story is surrounded by contradictory legends, on none of which reliance can be placed. Some of these emanate from a Hindu, some from a Mohammedan source, and claim him by turns as a Sûfî and a Brâhman saint. His name, however, is practically a conclusive proof of Moslem ancestry: and the most probable tale is that which represents him as the actual or adopted child of a Mohammedan weaver of Benares, the city in which the chief events of his life took place.

In fifteenth-century Benares the syncretistic tendencies of Bhakti religion had reached full development. Sûfîs and Brâhmans appear to have met in disputation: the most spiritual members of both creeds frequenting the teachings of Râmânanda, whose reputation was then at its height. The boy Kabîr, in whom the religious passion was innate, saw in Râmânanda his destined teacher; but knew how slight were the chances that a Hindu guru would accept a Mohammedan as disciple. He therefore hid upon the steps of the river Ganges, where Râmânanda was accustomed to bathe; with the result that the master, coming down to the water, trod upon his body unexpectedly, and exclaimed in his astonishment, "Ram! Ram!"—the name of the incarnation under which he worshipped God. Kabîr then declared that he had received the mantra of initiation from Râmânanda's lips, and was by it admitted to discipleship. In spite of the protests of orthodox Brâhmans and Mohammedans, both equally annoyed by this contempt of theological landmarks, he persisted in his claim; thus exhibiting in action that very principle of religious synthesis which Râmânanda had sought to establish in thought. Râmânanda appears to have accepted him, and though Mohammedan legends speak of the famous Sûfî Pîr, Takkî of Jhansî, as Kabîr's master in later life, the Hindu saint is the only human teacher to whom in his songs he acknowledges indebtedness.

The little that we know of Kabîr's life contradicts many current ideas concerning the Oriental mystic. Of the stages of discipline through which he passed, the manner in which his spiritual genius developed, we are completely ignorant. He seems to have remained for years the disciple of Râmânanda, joining in the theological and philosophical arguments which his master held with all the great Mullahs and Brâhmans of his day; and to this source we may perhaps trace his acquaintance with the terms of Hindu and Sûfî philosophy. He may or may not have submitted to the traditional education of the Hindu or the Sûfî contemplative: it is clear, at any rate, that he never adopted the life of the professional ascetic, or retired from the world in order to devote himself to bodily mortifications and the exclusive pursuit of the contemplative life. Side by side with his interior life of adoration, its artistic expression in music and words—for he was a skilled musician as well as a poet—he lived the sane and diligent life of the Oriental craftsman. All the legends agree on this point: that Kabîr was a weaver, a simple and unlettered man, who earned his living at the loom. Like Paul the tentmaker, Boehme the cobbler, Bunyan the tinker, Tersteegen the ribbon-maker, he knew how to combine vision and industry; the work of his hands helped rather than hindered the impassioned meditation of his heart. Hating mere bodily austerities, he was no ascetic, but a married man, the father of a family—a circumstance which Hindu legends of the monastic type vainly attempt to conceal or explain—and it was from out of the heart of the common life that he sang his rapturous lyrics of divine love. Here his works corroborate the traditional story of his life. Again and again he extols the life of home, the value and reality of diurnal existence, with its opportunities for love and renunciation; pouring contempt—upon the professional sanctity of the Yogi, who "has a great beard and matted locks, and looks like a goat," and on all who think it necessary to flee a world pervaded by love, joy, and beauty—the proper theatre of man's quest—in order to find that One Reality Who has "spread His form of love throughout all the world."[1]

It does not need much experience of ascetic literature to recognize the boldness and originality of this attitude in such a time and place. From the point of view of orthodox sanctity, whether Hindu or Mohammedan, Kabîr was plainly a heretic; and his frank dislike of all institutional religion, all external observance—which was as thorough and as intense as that of the Quakers themselves—completed, so far as ecclesiastical opinion was concerned, his reputation as a dangerous man. The "simple union" with Divine Reality which he perpetually extolled, as alike the duty and the joy of every soul, was independent both of ritual and of bodily austerities; the God whom he proclaimed was "neither in Kaaba nor in Kailâsh." Those who sought Him needed not to go far; for He awaited discovery everywhere, more accessible to "the washerwoman and the carpenter" than to the self—righteous holy man.[2] Therefore the whole apparatus of piety, Hindu and Moslem alike—the temple and mosque, idol and holy water, scriptures and priests—were denounced by this inconveniently clear-sighted poet as mere substitutes for reality; dead things intervening between the soul and its love—

> The images are all lifeless, they cannot speak:
> I know, for I have cried aloud to them.
> The Purâna and the Koran are mere words:
> lifting up the curtain, I have seen.[3]

This sort of thing cannot be tolerated by any organized church; and it is not surprising that Kabîr, having his head-quarters in Benares, the very centre of

[1] Cf. Poems Nos. XXI, XL, XLIII, LXVI, LXXVI.

[2] Poems I, II, XLI.

[3] Poems XLII, LXV, LXVII.

priestly influence, was subjected to considerable persecution. The well-known legend of the beautiful courtesan sent by Brâhmans to tempt his virtue, and converted, like the Magdalen, by her sudden encounter with the initiate of a higher love, pre serves the memory of the fear and dislike with which he was regarded by the ecclesiastical powers. Once at least, after the performance of a supposed miracle of healing, he was brought before the Emperor Sikandar Lodi, and charged with claiming the possession of divine powers. But Sikandar Lodi, a ruler of considerable culture, was tolerant of the eccentricities of saintly persons belonging to his own faith. Kabîr, being of Mohammedan birth, was outside the authority of the Brâhmans, and technically classed with the Sûfîs, to whom great theological latitude was allowed. Therefore, though he was banished in the interests of peace from Benares, his life was spared. This seems to have happened in 1495, when he was nearly sixty years of age; it is the last event in his career of which we have definite knowledge. Thenceforth he appears to have moved about amongst various cities of northern India, the centre of a group of disciples; continuing in exile that life of apostle and poet of love to which, as he declares in one of his songs, he was destined "from the beginning of time." In 1518, an old man, broken in health, and with hands so feeble that he could no longer make the music which he loved, he died at Maghar near Gorakhpur.

A beautiful legend tells us that after his death his Mohammedan and Hindu disciples disputed the possession of his body; which the Mohammedans wished to bury, the Hindus to burn. As they argued together, Kabîr appeared before them, and told them to lift the shroud and look at that which lay beneath. They did so, and found in the place of the corpse a heap of flowers; half of which were buried by the Mohammedans at Maghar, and half carried by the Hindus to the holy city of Benares to be burned—fitting conclusion to a life which had made fragrant the most beautiful doctrines of two great creeds.

II

The poetry of mysticism might be defined on the one hand as a temperamental reaction to the vision of Reality: on the other, as a form of prophecy. As it is the special vocation of the mystical consciousness to mediate between two orders, going out in loving adoration towards God and coming home to tell the secrets of Eternity to other men; so the artistic self-expression of this consciousness has also a double character. It is love-poetry, but love-poetry which is often written with a missionary intention.

Kabîr's songs are of this kind: out-births at once of rapture and of charity. Written in the popular Hindi, not in the literary tongue, they were deliberately addressed—like the vernacular poetry of Jacopone da Todì and Richard Rolle—to the people rather than to the professionally religious class; and all must be struck by the constant employment in them of imagery drawn from the common life, the universal experience. It is by the simplest metaphors, by constant appeals to needs, passions, relations which all men understand—the bridegroom and bride, the guru and disciple, the pilgrim, the farmer, the migrant bird— that he drives home his intense conviction of the reality of the soul's intercourse with the Transcendent. There are in his universe no fences between the "natural" and "supernatural" worlds; everything is a part of the creative Play of God, and therefore—even in its humblest details—capable of revealing the Player's mind.

This willing acceptance of the here-and-now as a means of representing supernal realities is a trait common to the greatest mystics. For them, when they have achieved at last the true theopathetic state, all aspects of the universe possess equal authority as sacramental declarations of the Presence of God; and their fearless employment of homely and physical symbols—often startling and even revolting to the unaccustomed taste—is in direct proportion to the exaltation of their spiritual life. The works of the great Sûfîs, and amongst the Christians of Jacopone da Todì, Ruysbroeck, Boehme, abound in illustrations of this law. Therefore we must not be surprised to find in Kabîr's songs—his desperate attempts to communicate his ecstasy and persuade other men to share it—a constant juxtaposition of concrete and metaphysical language; swift alternations between the most intensely anthropomorphic, the most subtly philosophical, ways of apprehending man's communion with the Divine. The need for this alternation, and its entire naturalness for the mind which employs it, is rooted in his concept, or vision, of the Nature of God; and unless we make some attempt to grasp this, we shall not go far in our understanding of his poems.

Kabîr belongs to that small group of supreme mystics—amongst whom St. Augustine, Ruysbroeck, and the Sûfî poet Jalâlu'ddîn Rûmî are perhaps the chief—who have achieved that which we might call the synthetic vision of God. These have resolved the perpetual opposition between the personal and impersonal, the transcendent and immanent, static and dynamic aspects of the Divine Nature; between the Absolute of philosophy and the "sure true Friend" of devotional religion. They have done this, not by taking these apparently incompatible concepts one after the other; but by ascending to a height of spiritual intuition at which they are, as Ruysbroeck said, "melted and merged in the Unity," and perceived as the completing opposites of a perfect Whole. This proceeding entails for them—and both Kabîr and Ruysbroeck expressly acknowledge it—a universe of three orders: Becoming, Being, and that which is "More than Being," i.e., God.[4] God is here felt to be not the final abstraction, but the one actuality. He inspires, supports, indeed inhabits, both the durational, conditioned, finite world of Becoming and the unconditioned, non-successional, infinite world of Being; yet utterly transcends them both. He is the omnipresent Reality, the "All-pervading" within Whom "the worlds are being told like beads." In His personal aspect He is the "beloved Fakir," teaching and companioning each soul. Considered as Immanent Spirit, He is "the Mind within the mind." But all these are at best partial aspects of His nature, mutually corrective: as the Persons in the Christian doctrine of the Trinity—to which this theological diagram bears a striking resemblance—represent different and compensating experiences of the Divine Unity within which they are resumed. As Ruysbroeck discerned a plane of reality upon which "we can speak no more of Father, Son, and Holy Spirit, but only of One Being, the very substance of the Divine Persons"; so Kabîr says that "beyond both the limited and the limitless is

[4] Nos. VII and XLIX.

He, the Pure Being."[5]

Brahma, then, is the Ineffable Fact compared with which "the distinction of the Conditioned from the Unconditioned is but a word": at once the utterly transcendent One of Absolutist philosophy, and the personal Lover of the individual soul—"common to all and special to each," as one Christian mystic has it. The need felt by Kabîr for both these ways of describing Reality is a proof of the richness and balance of his spiritual experience; which neither cosmic nor anthropomorphic symbols, taken alone, could express. More absolute than the Absolute, more personal than the human mind, Brahma therefore exceeds whilst He includes all the concepts of philosophy, all the passionate intuitions of the heart. He is the Great Affirmation, the font of energy, the source of life and love, the unique satisfaction of desire. His creative word is the *Om* or "Everlasting Yea." The negative philosophy which strips from the Divine Nature all Its attributes and defining Him only by that which He is not—reduces Him to an "Emptiness," is abhorrent to this most vital of poets.—Brahma, he says, "may never be found in abstractions." He is the One Love who Pervades the world., discerned in His fullness only by the eyes of love; and those who know Him thus share, though they may never tell, the joyous and ineffable secret of the universe.[6]

Now Kabîr, achieving this synthesis between the personal and cosmic aspects of the Divine Nature, eludes the three great dangers which threaten mystical religion.

First, he escapes the excessive emotionalism, the tendency to an exclusively anthropomorphic devotion, which results from an unrestricted cult of Divine Personality, especially under an incarnational form; seen in India in the exaggerations of Krishna worship, in Europe in the sentimental extravagances of certain Christian saints.

Next, he is protected from the soul-destroying conclusions of pure monism, inevitable if its logical implications are pressed home: that is, the identity of substance between God and the soul, with its corollary of the total absorption of that soul in the Being of God as the goal of the spiritual life. For the thorough-going monist the soul, in so far as it is real, is substantially identical with God; and the true object of existence is the making patent of this latent identity, the realization which finds expression in the Vedântist formula "That art thou." But Kabîr says that Brahma and the creature are "ever distinct, yet ever united"; that the wise man knows the spiritual as well as the material world to "be no more than His footstool."[7] The soul's union with Him is a love union, a mutual inhabitation; that essentially dualistic relation which all mystical religion expresses, not a self-mergence which leaves no place for personality. This eternal distinction, the mysterious union-in-separateness of God and the soul, is a necessary doctrine of all sane mysticism; for no scheme which fails to find a place for it can represent more than a fragment of that soul's intercourse with the spiritual world. Its affirmation was one of the distinguishing features of the Vaishnavite reformation preached by

[5] No. VII.
[6] Nos. VII, XXVI, LXXVI, XC.
[7] Nos. VII and IX.

Râmânuja; the principle of which had descended through Râmânanda to Kabîr.

Last, the warmly human and direct apprehension of God as the supreme Object of love, the soul's comrade, teacher, and bridegroom, which is so passionately and frequently expressed in Kabîr's poems, balances and controls those abstract tendencies which are inherent in the metaphysical side of his vision of Reality: and prevents it from degenerating into that sterile worship of intellectual formulæ which became the curse of the Vedântist school. For the mere intellectualist, as for the mere pietist, he has little approbation.[8] Love is throughout his "absolute sole Lord": the unique source of the more abundant life which he enjoys, and the common factor which unites the finite and infinite worlds. All is soaked in love: that love which he described in almost Johannine language as the "Form of God." The whole of creation is the Play of the Eternal Lover; the living, changing, growing expression of Brahma's love and joy. As these twin passions preside over the generation of human life, so "beyond the mists of pleasure and pain" Kabîr finds them governing the creative acts of God. His manifestation is love; His activity is joy. Creation springs from one glad act of affirmation: the Everlasting Yea, perpetually uttered within the depths of the Divine Nature.[9] In accordance with this concept of the universe as a Love-Game which eternally goes forward, a progressive manifestation of Brahma—one of the many notions which he adopted from the common stock of Hindu religious ideas, and illuminated by his poetic genius—movement, rhythm, perpetual change, forms an integral part of Kabîr's vision of Reality. Though the Eternal and Absolute is ever present to his consciousness, yet his concept of the Divine Nature is essentially dynamic. It is by the symbols of motion that he most often tries to convey it to us: as in his constant reference to dancing, or the strangely modern picture of that Eternal Swing of the Universe which is "held by the cords of love."[10]

It is a marked characteristic of mystical literature that the great contemplatives, in their effort to convey to us the nature of their communion with the supersensuous, are inevitably driven to employ some form of sensuous imagery: coarse and inaccurate as they know such imagery to be, even at the best. Our normal human consciousness is so completely committed to dependence on the senses, that the fruits of intuition itself are instinctively referred to them. In that intuition it seems to the mystics that all the dim cravings and partial apprehensions of sense find perfect fulfilment. Hence their constant declaration that they *see* the uncreated light, they *hear* the celestial melody, they *taste* the sweetness of the Lord, they know an ineffable fragrance, they feel the very contact of love. "Him verily seeing and fully feeling, Him spiritually hearing and Him delectably smelling and sweetly swallowing," as Julian of Norwich has it. In those amongst them who develop psycho-sensorial automatisms, these parallels between sense and spirit may present themselves to consciousness in the form of hallucinations: as the light seen by Suso, the music heard by Rolle, the celestial perfumes which filled St. Catherine of Siena's cell, the physical wounds felt by St. Francis and St. Teresa. These are exces-

[8] Cf. especially Nos. LIX, LXVII, LXXV, XC, XCI.

[9] Nos. XVII, XXVI, LXXVI, LXXXII.

[10] No. XVI.

sive dramatizations of the symbolism under which the mystic tends instinctively to represent his spiritual intuition to the surface consciousness. Here, in the special sense-perception which he feels to be most expressive of Reality, his peculiar idiosyncrasies come out.

Now Kabîr, as we might expect in one whose reactions to the spiritual order were so wide and various, uses by turn all the symbols of sense. He tells us that he has "seen without sight" the effulgence of Brahma, tasted the divine nectar, felt the ecstatic contact of Reality, smelt the fragrance of the heavenly flowers. But he was essentially a poet and musician: rhythm and harmony were to him the garments of beauty and truth. Hence in his lyrics he shows himself to be, like Richard Rolle, above all things a musical mystic. Creation, he says again and again, is full of music: it *is* music. At the heart of the Universe "white music is blossoming": love weaves the melody, whilst renunciation beats the time. It can be heard in the home as well as in the heavens; discerned by the ears of common men as well as by the trained senses of the ascetic. Moreover, the body of every man is a lyre on which Brahma, "the source of all music," plays. Everywhere Kabîr discerns the "Unstruck Music of the Infinite"—that celestial melody which the angel played to St. Francis, that ghostly symphony which filled the soul of Rolle with ecstatic joy.[11] The one figure which he adopts from the Hindu Pantheon and constantly uses, is that of Krishna the Divine Flute Player.[12] He sees the supernal music, too, in its visual embodiment, as rhythmical movement: that mysterious dance of the universe before the face of Brahma, which is at once an act of worship and an expression of the infinite rapture of the Immanent God.'

Yet in this wide and rapturous vision of the universe Kabîr never loses touch with diurnal existence, never forgets the common life. His feet are firmly planted upon earth; his lofty and passionate apprehensions are perpetually controlled by the activity of a sane and vigorous intellect, by the alert commonsense so often found in persons of real mystical genius. The constant insistence on simplicity and directness, the hatred of all abstractions and philosophizings,[13] the ruthless criticism of external religion: these are amongst his most marked characteristics. God is the Root whence all manifestations, "material" and "spiritual," alike proceed;[14] and God is the only need of man—"happiness shall be yours when you come to the Root."[15] Hence to those who keep their eye on the "one thing needful," denominations, creeds, ceremonies, the conclusions of philosophy, the disciplines of asceticism, are matters of comparative indifference. They represent merely the different angles from which the soul may approach that simple union with Brahma which is its goal; and are useful only in so faras they contribute to this consummation. So thorough-going is Kabîr's eclecticism, that he seems by turns Vedântist and Vaishnavite, Pantheist and Transcendentalist, Brâhman and Sûfî. In the effort to tell the truth about that ineffable apprehension, so vast and yet so near, which

[11] Nos. XVII, XVIII, XXXIX, XLI, LIV, LXXVI, LXXXIII, LXXXIX, XCVII.
[12] Nos. L, LIII, LXVIII.
[13] Nos. XXVI, XXXII, LXXVI.
[14] Nos. LXXV, LXXVIII, LXXX, XC.
[15] No. LXXX.

controls his life, he seizes and twines together—as he might have woven together contrasting threads upon his loom—symbols and ideas drawn from the most violent and conflicting philosophies and faiths. All are needed, if he is ever to suggest the character of that One whom the Upanishad called "the Sun-coloured Being who is beyond this Darkness": as all the colours of the spectrum are needed if we would demonstrate the simple richness of white light. In thus adapting traditional materials to his own use he follows a method common amongst the mystics; who seldom exhibit any special love for originality of form. They will pour their wine into almost any vessel that comes to hand: generally using by preference—and lifting to new levels of beauty and significance—the religious or philosophic formulæ current in their own day. Thus we find that some of Kabîr's finest poems have as their subjects the commonplaces of Hindu philosophy and religion: the Lîlâ or Sport of God, the Ocean of Bliss, the Bird of the Soul, Mâyâ, the Hundred-petalled Lotus, and the "Formless Form." Many, again, are soaked in Sûfî imagery and feeling. Others use as their material the ordinary surroundings and incidents of Indian life: the temple bells, the ceremony of the lamps, marriage, suttee, pilgrimage, the characters of the seasons; all felt by him in their mystical aspect, as sacraments of the soul's relation with Brahma. In many of these a particularly beautiful and intimate feeling for Nature is shown.[16]

In the collection of songs here translated there will be found examples which illustrate nearly every aspect of Kabîr's thought, and all the fluctuations of the mystic's emotion: the ecstasy, the despair, the still beatitude, the eager self-devotion, the flashes of wide illumination, the moments of intimate love. His wide and deep vision of the universe, the "Eternal Sport" of creation (LXXXII), the worlds being "told like beads" within the Being of God (XIV, XVI, XVII, LXXVI), is here seen balanced by his lovely and delicate sense of intimate communion with the Divine Friend, Lover, Teacher of the soul (X, XI, XXIII, XXXV, LI, LXXXV, LXXXVI, LXXXVIII, XCII, XCIII; above all, the beautiful poem XXXIV). As these apparently paradoxical views of Reality are resolved in Brâhma, so all other opposites are reconciled in Him: bondage and liberty, love and renunciation, pleasure and pain (XVII, XXV, XL, LXXIX). Union with Him is the one thing that matters to the soul, its destiny and its need (LI, I, II, LIV, LXX, LXXIV, XCIII, XCVI); and this union, this discovery of God, is the simplest and most natural of all things, if we would but grasp it (XLI, XLVI, LVI, LXXII, LXXVI, LXXVIII, XCVII). The union, however, is brought about by love, not by knowledge or ceremonial observances (XXXVIII, LIV, LV, LIX, XCI); and the apprehension which that union confers is ineffable—"neither This nor That," as Ruysbroeck has it (IX, XLVI, LXXVI). Real worship and communion is in Spirit and in Truth (XL, XLI, LVI, LXIII, LXV, LXX), therefore idolatry is an insult to the Divine Lover (XLII, LXIX) and the devices of professional sanctity are useless apart from charity and purity of soul (LIV, LXV, LXVI). Since all things, and especially the heart of man, are God-inhabited, God-possessed (XXVI, LVI, LXXVI, LXXXIX, XCVII), He may best be found in the here-and-now: in the normal. human, bodily existence, the "mud" of material life (III, IV, VI, XXI, XXXIX, XL, XLIII, XLVIII, LXXII). "We can reach the goal without crossing the road" (LXXVI)—not the cloister but the home is the proper theatre

[16] Nos. XV, XXIII, LXVII, LXXXVII, XCVII.

of man's efforts: and if he cannot find God there, he need not hope for success by going farther afield. "In the home is reality." There love and detachment, bondage and freedom, joy and pain play by turns upon the soul; and it is from their conflict that the Unstruck Music of the Infinite proceeds. Kabîr says: "None but Brahma can evoke its melodies."

III

"This version of Kabîr's songs is chiefly the work of Mr. Rabîndranâth Tagore, the trend of whose mystical genius makes him—as all who read these poems will see—a peculiarly sympathetic interpreter of Kabîr's vision and thought. It has been based upon the printed Hindî text with Bengali translation of Mr. Kshiti Mohan Sen; who has gathered from many sources—sometimes from books and manuscripts, sometimes from the lips of wandering ascetics and minstrels—a large collection of poems and hymns to which Kabîr's name is attached, and carefully sifted the authentic songs from the many spurious works now attributed to him. These painstaking labours alone have made the present undertaking possible.

We have also had before us a manuscript English translation of 116 songs made by Mr. Ajit Kumâr Chakravarty from Mr. Kshiti Mohan Sen's text, and a prose essay upon Kabîr from the same hand. From these we have derived great assistance. A considerable number of readings from the translation have been adopted by us; whilst several of the facts mentioned in the essay have been incorporated into this introduction. Our most grateful thanks are due to Mr. Ajit Kumar Chakravarty for the extremely generous and unselfish manner in which he has placed his work at our disposal.

E. U.

KABIR'S POEMS

I

I. 13. *mo ko kahân dhûnro bande*

O servant, where dost thou seek Me?
Lo! I am beside thee.
I am neither in temple nor in mosque: I am neither in Kaaba nor in Kailash:
Neither am I in rites and ceremonies, nor in Yoga and renunciation.
If thou art a true seeker, thou shalt at once see Me:
thou shalt meet Me in a moment of time.
Kabîr says, "O Sadhu! God is the breath of all breath."

II

I. 16. *Santan jât na pûcho nirguniyân*

It is needless to ask of a saint the caste to which he belongs;
For the priest, the warrior. the tradesman, and all the
thirty-six castes, alike are seeking for God.
It is but folly to ask what the caste of a saint may be;
The barber has sought God, the washerwoman, and the carpenter—
Even Raidas was a seeker after God.
The Rishi Swapacha was a tanner by caste.
Hindus and Moslems alike have achieved that End, where remains no
mark of distinction.

III

I. 57. *sâdho bhâî, jîval hî karo âs›â*

O friend! hope for Him whilst you live, know whilst you live,
understand whilst you live: for in life deliverance abides.
If your bonds be not broken whilst living, what hope of
deliverance in death?
It is but an empty dream, that the soul shall have union with Him
because it has passed from the body:
If He is found now, He is found then,
If not, we do but go to dwell in the City of Death.
If you have union now, you shall have it hereafter.
Bathe in the truth, know the true Guru, have faith in the true Name!

Kabîr says: "It is the Spirit of the quest which helps; I am the slave of this Spirit of the quest."

IV

I. 58. *bâgo nâ jâ re nâ jâ*

Do not go to the garden of flowers!
O Friend! go not there;
In your body is the garden of flowers.
Take your seat on the thousand petals of the lotus, and there gaze on the Infinite Beauty.

V

I. 63. *avadhû, mâyâ tajî na jây*

Tell me, Brother, how can I renounce Maya?
When I gave up the tying of ribbons, still I tied my garment about me:
When I gave up tying my garment, still I covered my body in its folds.
So, when I give up passion, I see that anger remains;
And when I renounce anger, greed is with me still;
And when greed is vanquished, pride and vainglory remain;
When the mind is detached and casts Maya away, still it clings to the letter.
Kabîr says, "Listen to me, dear Sadhu! the true path is rarely found."

VI

I. 83. *candâ jhalkai yahi ghat mâhîn*

The moon shines in my body, but my blind eyes cannot see it:
The moon is within me, and so is the sun.
The unstruck drum of Eternity is sounded within me;
but my deaf ears cannot hear it.

So long as man clamours for the *I* and the *Mine,*
his works are as naught:
When all love of the *I* and the *Mine* is dead, then
the work of the Lord is done.
For work has no other aim than the getting of knowledge:
When that comes, then work is put away.

The flower blooms for the fruit:
when the fruit comes, the flower withers.
The musk is in the deer, but it seeks it not within itself:
it wanders in quest of grass.

VII

I. 85. *Sâdho, Brahm alakh lakhâyâ*

When He Himself reveals Himself, Brahma brings into manifestation

That which can never be seen.
As the seed is in the plant, as the shade is in the tree,
as the void is in the sky, as infinite forms are in the void—
So from beyond the Infinite, the Infinite comes; and from the
Infinite the finite extends.

The creature is in Brahma, and Brahma is in the creature:
they are ever distinct, yet ever united.
He Himself is the tree, the seed, and the germ.
He Himself is the flower, the fruit, and the shade.
He Himself is the sun, the light, and the lighted.
He Himself is Brahma, creature, and Maya.
He Himself is the manifold form, the infinite space;
He is the breath, the word, and the meaning.
He Himself is the limit and the limitless:
and beyond both the limited and the limitless is He, the Pure Being.
He is the Immanent Mind in Brahma and in the creature.

The Supreme Soul is seen within the soul,
The Point is seen within the Supreme Soul,
And within the Point, the reflection is seen again.
Kabîr is blest because he has this supreme vision!

VIII

I. 101. *is ghat antar bâg bagîce*

Within this earthen vessel are bowers and groves,
and within it is the Creator:
Within this vessel are the seven oceans and the unnumbered stars.
The touchstone and the jewel-appraiser are within;
And within this vessel the Eternal soundeth, and the spring wells up.
Kabîr says: "Listen to me, my Friend! My beloved Lord is within."

IX

I. 104. *aisâ lo nahîn taisâ lo*

O How may I ever express that secret word?
O how can I say He is not like this, and He is like that?
If I say that He is within me, the universe is ashamed:
If I say that He is without me, it is falsehood.
He makes the inner and the outer worlds to be indivisibly one;
The conscious and the unconscious, both are His footstools.
He is neither manifest nor hidden, He is neither revealed nor unrevealed:
There are no words to tell that which He is.

X

I. 121. *tohi mori lagan lagâye re phakîr wâ*

To Thee Thou hast drawn my love, O Fakir!
I was sleeping in my own chamber, and Thou didst awaken me;
striking me with Thy voice, O Fakir!
I was drowning in the deeps of the ocean of this world, and
Thou didst save me: upholding me with Thine arm, O Fakir!
Only one word and no second—and
Thou hast made me tear off all my bonds, O Fakir!
Kabîr says, "Thou hast united Thy heart to my heart, O Fakir!"

XI

I. 131. *nis' din khelat rahî sakhiyân sang*

I played day and night with my comrades, and now I am greatly afraid.
So high is my Lord's palace, my heart trembles to mount its stairs:
yet I must not be shy, if I would enjoy His love.
My heart must cleave to my Lover; I must withdraw my veil,
and meet Him with all my body:
Mine eyes must perform the ceremony of the lamps of love.
Kabîr says: "Listen to me, friend: he understands who loves.
If you feel not love's longing for your Beloved One, it is vain
to adorn your body, vain to put unguent on your eyelids."

XII

II. 24. *hamsâ, kaho purâtan vât*

Tell me, O Swan, your ancient tale.
From what land do you come, O Swan? to what shore will you fly?
Where would you take your rest, O Swan, and what do you seek?

Even this morning, O Swan, awake, arise, follow me!
There is a land where no doubt nor sorrow have rule:
where the terror of Death is no more.
There the woods of spring are a-bloom, and the fragrant scent
"He is I" is borne on the wind:
There the bee of the heart is deeply immersed, and desires no other joy.

XIII

II. 37. *angadhiyâ devâ*

O Lord Increate, who will serve Thee?
Every votary offers his worship to the God of his own creation:
each day he receives service—
None seek Him, the Perfect: Brahma, the Indivisible Lord.
They believe in ten Avatars; but no Avatar can be the Infinite Spirit,

for he suffers the results of his deeds:
The Supreme One must be other than this.
The Yogi, the Sanyasi, the Ascetics, are disputing one with another:
Kabîr says, "O brother! he who has seen that radiance of love, he is saved."

XIV

II. 56. *dariyâ kî lahar dariyâo hai jî*

The river and its waves are one
surf: where is the difference between the river and its waves?
When the wave rises, it is the water; and when it falls, it is
the same water again. Tell me, Sir, where is the distinction?
Because it has been named as wave, shall it no longer be
considered as water?

Within the Supreme Brahma, the worlds are being told like beads:
Look upon that rosary with the eyes of wisdom.

XV

II. 57. *jânh khelat vasant riturâj*

Where Spring, the lord of the seasons, reigneth,
there the Unstruck Music sounds of itself,
There the streams of light flow in all directions;
Few are the men who can cross to that shore!
There, where millions of Krishnas stand with hands folded,
Where millions of Vishnus bow their heads,
Where millions of Brahmâs are reading the Vedas,
Where millions of Shivas are lost in contemplation,
Where millions of Indras dwell in the sky,
Where the demi-gods and the munis are unnumbered,
Where millions of Saraswatis, Goddess of Music, play on the vina—
There is my Lord self-revealed: and the scent of sandal and
flowers dwells in those deeps.

XVI

II. 59. *jânh, cet acet khambh dôû*

Between the poles of the conscious and the unconscious,
there has the mind made a swing:
Thereon hang all beings and all worlds,
and that swing never ceases its sway.
Millions of beings are there: the sun and the moon in their courses are there:
Millions of ages pass, and the swing goes on.
All swing! the sky and the earth and the air and the water;
and the Lord Himself taking form:
And the sight of this has made Kabîr a servant.

XVII

II. 61. *grah candra tapan jot varat hai*

The light of the sun, the moon, and the stars shines bright:
The melody of love swells forth, and the rhythm of love's detachment beats the time.
Day and night, the chorus of music fills the heavens; and Kabîr says "My Beloved One gleams like the lightning flash in the sky."

Do you know how the moments perform their adoration?
Waving its row of lamps, the universe sings in worship day and night,
There are the hidden banner and the secret canopy:
There the sound of the unseen bells is heard.
Kabîr says: "There adoration never ceases;
there the Lord of the Universe sitteth on His throne."
The whole world does its works and commits its errors:
but few are the lovers who know the Beloved.
The devout seeker is he who mingles in his heart
the double currents of love and detachment,
like the mingling of the streams of Ganges and Jumna;
In his heart the sacred water flows day and night;
and thus the round of births and deaths is brought to an end.

Behold what wonderful rest is in the Supreme Spirit!
and he enjoys it, who makes himself meet for it.
Held by the cords of love, the swing of the Ocean of Joy sways to and fro; and a mighty sound breaks forth in song.
See what a lotus blooms there without water! and Kabîr says "My heart's bee drinks its nectar."
What a wonderful lotus it is, that blooms at the heart of the spinning wheel of the universe!
Only a few pure souls know of its true delight.
Music is all around it, and there the heart partakes of the joy of the Infinite Sea.
Kabîr says: "Dive thou into that Ocean of sweetness: thus let all errors of life and of death flee away."

Behold how the thirst of the five senses is quenched there! and the three forms of misery are no more!
Kabîr says: "It is the sport of the Unattainable One: look within, and behold how the moon-beams of that Hidden One shine in you."
There falls the rhythmic beat of life and death:
Rapture wells forth, and all space is radiant with light.
There the Unstruck Music is sounded; it is the music of the love of the three worlds.
There millions of lamps of sun and of moon are burning;
There the drum beats, and the lover swings in play.

There love-songs resound, and light rains in showers; and the worshipper is entranced in the taste of the heavenly nectar.
Look upon life and death; there is no separation between them,
The right hand and the left hand are one and the same.
Kabîr says: "There the wise man is speechless; for this truth may never be found in Vadas or in books."

I have had my Seat on the Self-poised One,
I have drunk of the Cup of the Ineffable,
I have found the Key of the Mystery,
I have reached the Root of Union.
Travelling by no track, I have come to the Sorrowless Land: very easily has the mercy of the great Lord come upon me.
They have sung of Him as infinite and unattainable: but I in my meditations have seen Him without sight.
That is indeed the sorrowless land, and none know the path that leads there:
Only he who is on that path has surely transcended all sorrow.
Wonderful is that land of rest, to which no merit can win;
It is the wise who has seen it, it is the wise who has sung of it.
This is the Ultimate Word: but can any express its marvellous savour?
He who has savoured it once, he knows what joy it can give.
Kabîr says: "Knowing it, the ignorant man becomes wise, and the wise man becomes speechless and silent,
The worshipper is utterly inebriated,
His wisdom and his detachment are made perfect;
He drinks from the cup of the inbreathings and the outbreathings of love."

There the whole sky is filled with sound, and there that music is made without fingers and without strings;
There the game of pleasure and pain does not cease.
Kabîr says: "If you merge your life in the Ocean of Life, you will find your life in the Supreme Land of Bliss."

What a frenzy of ecstasy there is in every hour! and the worshipper is pressing out and drinking the essence of the hours: he lives in the life of Brahma.
I speak truth, for I have accepted truth in life; I am now attached to truth, I have swept all tinsel away.
Kabîr says: "Thus is the worshipper set free from fear; thus have all errors of life and of death left him."

There the sky is filled with music:
There it rains nectar:
There the harp-strings jingle, and there the drums beat.
What a secret splendour is there, in the mansion of the sky!
There no mention is made of the rising and the setting of the sun;
In the ocean of manifestation, which is the light of love, day

and night are felt to be one.
Joy for ever, no sorrow, — no struggle!
There have I seen joy filled to the brim, perfection of joy;
No place for error is there.
Kabîr says: "There have I witnessed the sport of One Bliss!"

I have known in my body the sport of the universe: I have escaped from the error of this world..
The inward and the outward are become as one sky, the Infinite and the finite are united: I am drunken with the sight of this All!
This Light of Thine fulfils the universe: the lamp of love that burns on the salver of knowledge.
Kabîr says: "There error cannot enter, and the conflict of life and death is felt no more."

XVIII

II. 77. *maddh âkas' âp jahân baithe*

The middle region of the sky, wherein the spirit dwelleth, is radiant with the music of light;
There, where the pure and white music blossoms, my Lord takes His delight.
In the wondrous effulgence of each hair of His body, the brightness of millions of suns and of moons is lost.
On that shore there is a city, where the rain of nectar pours and pours, and never ceases.
Kabîr says: "Come, O Dharmadas! and see my great Lord's Durbar."

XIX

II. 20. *paramâtam guru nikat virâjatn*

O my heart! the Supreme Spirit, the great Master, is near you: wake, oh wake!
Run to the feet of your Beloved: for your Lord stands near to your head.
You have slept for unnumbered ages; this morning will you not wake?

XX

II. 22. *man tu pâr utar kânh jaiho*

To what shore would you cross, O my heart? there is no traveller before you, there is no road:
Where is the movement, where is the rest, on that shore?
There is no water; no boat, no boatman, is there;
There is not so much as a rope to tow the boat, nor a man to draw it.
No earth, no sky, no time, no thing, is there: no shore, no ford!
There, there is neither body nor mind: and where is the place

that shall still the thirst of the soul? You shall find naught
in that emptiness.
Be strong, and enter into your own body: for there your foothold
is firm. Consider it well, O my heart! go not elsewhere,
Kabîr says: "Put all imaginations away, and stand fast in that
which you are."

XXI

II. 33. *ghar ghar dîpak barai*

Lamps burn in every house, O blind one! and you cannot see them.
One day your eyes shall suddenly be opened, and you shall see:
and the fetters of death will fall from you.
There is nothing to say or to hear, there is nothing to do: it is
he who is living, yet dead, who shall never die again.

Because he lives in solitude, therefore the Yogi says that his home is far away.
Your Lord is near: yet you are climbing the palm-tree to seek Him.
The Brâhman priest goes from house to house and initiates people
into faith:
Alas! the true fountain of life is beside you., and you have set
up a stone to worship.
Kabîr says: "I may never express how sweet my Lord is. Yoga and
the telling of beads, virtue and vice—these are naught to Him."

XXII

II. 38. *Sâdho, so satgur mohi bhâwai*

O brother, my heart yearns for that true Guru, who fills the cup
of true love, and drinks of it himself, and offers it then to me.
He removes the veil from the eyes, and gives the true Vision of Brahma:
He reveals the worlds in Him, and makes me to hear the Unstruck Music:
He shows joy and sorrow to be one:
He fills all utterance with love.
Kabîr says: "Verily he has no fear, who has such a Guru to lead
him to the shelter of safety!"

XXIII

II. 40. *tinwir sâñjh kâ gahirâ âwai*

The shadows of evening fall thick and deep, and the darkness of
love envelops the body and the mind.
Open the window to the west, and be lost in the sky of love;
Drink the sweet honey that steeps the petals of the lotus of the heart.
Receive the waves in your body: what splendour is in the region of the sea!
Hark! the sounds of conches and bells are rising.
Kabîr says: "O brother, behold! the Lord is in this vessel of my body."

XXIV

II. 48. *jis se rahani apâr jagat men*

More than all else do I cherish at heart that love which makes me to live a limitless life in this world.
It is like the lotus, which lives in the water and blooms in the water: yet the water cannot touch its petals, they open beyond its reach.
It is like a wife, who enters the fire at the bidding of love.
She burns and lets others grieve, yet never dishonours love.
This ocean of the world is hard to cross: its waters are very deep. Kabîr says: "Listen to me, O Sadhu! few there are who have reached its end."

XXV

II. 45. *Hari ne apnâ âp chipâyâ*

My Lord hides Himself, and my Lord wonderfully reveals Himself:
My Lord has encompassed me with hardness, and my Lord has cast down my limitations.
My Lord brings to me words of sorrow and words of joy, and He Himself heals their strife.
I will offer my body and mind to my Lord: I will give up my life, but never can I forget my Lord!

XXVI

II. 75. *ônkâr siwae kôî sirjai*

All things are created by the Om;
The love-form is His body.
He is without form, without quality, without decay:
Seek thou union with Him!
But that formless God takes a thousand forms in the eyes of His creatures:
He is pure and indestructible,
His form is infinite and fathomless,
He dances in rapture, and waves of form arise from His dance.
The body and the mind cannot contain themselves, when they are touched by His great joy.
He is immersed in all consciousness, all joys, and all sorrows;
He has no beginning and no end;
He holds all within His bliss.

XXVII

II. 81. *satgur sôî dayâ kar dînhâ*

It is the mercy of my true Guru that has made me to know the unknown;
I have learned from Him how to walk without feet, to see without

eyes, to hear without ears, to drink without mouth, to fly without wings;
I have brought my love and my meditation into the land where
there is no sun and moon, nor day and night.
Without eating, I have tasted of the sweetness of nectar; and
without water, I have quenched my thirst.
Where there is the response of delight, there is the fullness of
joy. Before whom can that joy be uttered?
Kabîr says: "The Guru is great beyond words, and great is the
good fortune of the disciple."

XXVIII

II. 85. *nirgun âge sargun nâcai*

Before the Unconditioned, the Conditioned dances:
"Thou and I are one!" this trumpet proclaims.
The Guru comes, and bows down before the disciple:
This is the greatest of wonders.

XXIX

II. 87. *Kabîr kab se bhaye vairâgî*

Gorakhnath asks Kabîr:
"Tell me, O Kabîr, when did your vocation begin?
Where did your love have its rise?"
Kabîr answers:
"When He whose forms are manifold had not begun His play: when
there was no Guru, and no disciple: when the world was not
spread out: when the Supreme One was alone—
Then I became an ascetic; then, O Gorakh, my love was drawn to Brahma.
Brahma did not hold the crown on his head; the god Vishnu was not
anointed as king; the power of Shiva was still unborn; when I
was instructed in Yoga.

I became suddenly revealed in Benares, and Râmânanda illumined me;
I brought with me the thirst for the Infinite, and I have come
for the meeting with Him.
In simplicity will I unite with the Simple One; my love will surge up.
O Gorakh, march thou with His music!"

XXX

II. 95. *yâ tarvar men ek pakherû*

On this tree is a bird: it dances in the joy of life.
None knows where it is: and who knows what the burden of its
music may be?
Where the branches throw a deep shade, there does it have its
nest: and it comes in the evening and flies away in the morning,

and says not a word of that which it means.
None tell me of this bird that sings within me.
It is neither coloured nor colourless: it has neither form nor outline:
It sits in the shadow of love.
It dwells within the Unattainable, the Infinite, and the Eternal; and no one marks when it comes and goes.
Kabîr says: "O brother Sadhu! deep is the mystery. Let wise men seek to know where rests that bird."

XXXI

II. 100. *nis` din sâlai ghâw*

A sore pain troubles me day and night, and I cannot sleep;
I long for the meeting with my Beloved, and my father's house gives me pleasure no more.
The gates of the sky are opened, the temple is revealed:
I meet my husband, and leave at His feet the offering of my body and my mind.

XXXII

II. 103. *nâco re mero man, matta hoy*

Dance, my heart! dance to-day with joy.
The strains of love fill the days and the nights with music, and the world is listening to its melodies:
Mad with joy, life and death dance to the rhythm of this music.
The hills and the sea and the earth dance. The world of man dances in laughter and tears.
Why put on the robe of the monk, and live aloof from the world in lonely pride?
Behold! my heart dances in the delight of a hundred arts; and the Creator is well pleased.

XXXIII

II. 105. *man mast huâ tab kyon bole*

Where is the need of words, when love has made drunken the heart?
I have wrapped the diamond in my cloak; why open it again and again?
When its load was light, the pan of the balance went up: now it is full, where is the need for weighing?
The swan has taken its flight to the lake beyond the mountains; why should it search for the pools and ditches any more?
Your Lord dwells within you: why need your outward eyes be opened?
Kabîr says: "Listen, my brother! my Lord, who ravishes my eyes,

has united Himself with me."

XXXIV

II. 110. *mohi tohi lâgî kaise chute*

How could the love between Thee and me sever?
As the leaf of the lotus abides on the water: so thou art my Lord, and I am Thy servant.
As the night-bird Chakor gazes all night at the moon: so Thou art my Lord and I am Thy servant.
From the beginning until the ending of time, there is love between Thee and me; and how shall such love be extinguished?
Kabîr says: "As the river enters into the ocean, so my heart touches Thee."

XXXV

II. 113. *vâlam, âwo hamâre geh re*

My body and my mind are grieved for the want of Thee;
O my Beloved! come to my house.
When people say I am Thy bride, I am ashamed; for I have not touched Thy heart with my heart.
Then what is this love of mine? I have no taste for food, I have no sleep; my heart is ever restless within doors and without.
As water is to the thirsty, so is the lover to the bride. Who is there that will carry my news to my Beloved?
Kabîr is restless: he is dying for sight of Him.

XXXVI

II. 126. *jâg piyârî, ab kân sowai*

O friend, awake, and sleep no more!
The night is over and gone, would you lose your day also?
Others, who have wakened, have received jewels;
O foolish woman! you have lost all whilst you slept.
Your lover is wise, and you are foolish, O woman!
You never prepared the bed of your husband:
O mad one! you passed your time in silly play.
Your youth was passed in vain, for you did not know your Lord;
Wake, wake! See! your bed is empty: He left you in the night.
Kabîr says: "Only she wakes, whose heart is pierced with the arrow of His music."

XXXVII

I. 36. *sûr parkâs', tanh rain kahân pâiye*

Where is the night, when the sun is shining? If it is night,

then the sun withdraws its light. Where knowledge is, can ignorance endure?
If there be ignorance, then knowledge must die.
If there be lust, how can love be there? Where there is love, there is no lust.

Lay hold on your sword, and join in the fight. Fight, O my brother, as long as life lasts.
Strike off your enemy's head, and there make an end of him quickly: then come, and bow your head at your King's Durbar.
He who is brave, never forsakes the battle: he who flies from it is no true fighter.
In the field of this body a great war goes forward, against passion, anger, pride, and greed:
It is in the kingdom of truth, contentment and purity, that this battle is raging; and the sword that rings forth most loudly is the sword of His Name.
Kabîr says: "When a brave knight takes the field, a host of cowards is put to flight.
It is a hard fight and a weary one, this fight of the truth-seeker: for the vow of the truth-seeker is more hard than that of the warrior, or of the widowed wife who would follow her husband.
For the warrior fights for a few hours, and the widow's struggle with death is soon ended:
But the truth-seeker's battle goes on day and night, as long as life lasts it never ceases."

XXXVIII

I. 50. *bhram kâ tâlâ lagâ mahal re*

The lock of error shuts the gate, open it with the key of love:
Thus, by opening the door, thou shalt wake the Beloved.
Kabîr says: "O brother! do not pass by such good fortune as this."

XXXIX

I. 59. *sâdho, yah tan thâth tanvure ka*

O friend! this body is His lyre; He tightens its strings, and draws from it the melody of Brahma.
If the strings snap and the keys slacken, then to dust must this instrument of dust return:
Kabîr says: "None but Brahma can evoke its melodies."

XL

I. 65. *avadhû bhûle ko ghar lâwe*

He is dear to me indeed who can call back the wanderer to his
home. In the home is the true union, in the home is enjoyment
of life: why should I forsake my home and wander in the forest?
If Brahma helps me to realize truth, verily I will find both
bondage and deliverance in home.
He is dear to me indeed who has power to dive deep into Brahma;
whose mind loses itself with ease in His contemplation.
He is dear to me who knows Brahma, and can dwell on His supreme
truth in meditation; and who can play the melody of the
Infinite by uniting love and renunciation in life.
Kabîr says: "The home is the abiding place; in the home is
reality; the home helps to attain Him Who is real. So stay
where you are, and all things shall come to you in time."

XLI

I. 76. *santo, sahaj samâdh bhalî*

O sadhu! the simple union is the best. Since the day when I met
with my Lord, there has been no end to the sport of our love.
I shut not my eyes, I close not my ears, I do not mortify my
body;
I see with eyes open and smile, and behold His beauty everywhere:
I utter His Name, and whatever I see, it reminds me of Him;
whatever I do., it becomes His worship.
The rising and the setting are one to me; all contradictions are
solved.
Wherever I go, I move round Him,
All I achieve is His service:
When I lie down, I lie prostrate at His feet.

He is the only adorable one to me: I have none other.
My tongue has left off impure words, it sings His glory day and
night:
Whether I rise or sit down, I can never forget Him; for the
rhythm of His music beats in my ears.
Kabîr says: "My heart is frenzied, and I disclose in my soul what
is hidden. I am immersed in that one great bliss which
transcends all pleasure and pain."

XLII

I. 79. *tîrath men to sab pânî hai*

There is nothing but water at the holy bathing places; and I know
that they are useless, for I have bathed in them.
The images are all lifeless, they cannot speak; I know, for I
have cried aloud to them.
The Purana and the Koran are mere words; lifting up the curtain,

I have seen.
Kabîr gives utterance to the words of experience; and he knows very well that all other things are untrue.

XLIII

I. 82. *pânî vic mîn piyâsî*

I laugh when I hear that the fish in the water is thirsty:
You do not see that the Real is in your home, and you wander from forest to forest listlessly!
Here is the truth! Go where you will, to Benares or to Mathura; if you do not find your soul, the world is unreal to you.

XLIV

I. 93. *gagan math gaib nisân gade*

The Hidden Banner is planted in the temple of the sky; there the blue canopy decked with the moon and set with bright jewels is spread.
There the light of the sun and the moon is shining: still your mind to silence before that splendour.
Kabîr says: "He who has drunk of this nectar, wanders like one who is mad."

XLV

I. 97. *sâdho, ko hai kânh se âyo*

Who are you, and whence do you come?
Where dwells that Supreme Spirit, and how does He have His sport with all created things?
The fire is in the wood; but who awakens it suddenly? Then it turns to ashes, and where goes the force of the fire?
The true guru teaches that He has neither limit nor infinitude.
Kabîr says: "Brahma suits His language to the understanding of His hearer."

XLVI

I. 98. *sâdho, sahajai kâyâ s'odho*

O sadhu! purify your body in the simple way.
As the seed is within the banyan tree, and within the seed are the flowers, the fruits, and the shade:
So the germ is within the body, and within that germ is the body again.
The fire, the air, the water, the earth, and the aether; you cannot have these outside of Him.
O, Kazi, O Pundit, consider it well: what is there that is not in the soul?
The water-filled pitcher is placed upon water, it has water

within and without.
It should not be given a name, lest it call forth the error of dualism.
Kabîr says: "Listen to the Word, the Truth, which is your essence. He speaks the Word to Himself; and He Himself is the Creator."

XLVII

I. 102. *tarvar ek mûl vin thâdâ*

There is a strange tree, which stands without roots and bears fruits without blossoming;
It has no branches and no leaves, it is lotus all over.
Two birds sing there; one is the Guru, and the other the disciple:
The disciple chooses the manifold fruits of life and tastes them, and the Guru beholds him in joy.
What Kabîr says is hard to understand: "The bird is beyond seeking, yet it is most clearly visible. The Formless is in the midst of all forms. I sing the glory of forms."

XLVIII

I. 107. *calat mansâ acal kînhî*

I have stilled my restless mind, and my heart is radiant: for in Thatness I have seen beyond That-ness. In company I have seen the Comrade Himself.
Living in bondage, I have set myself free: I have broken away from the clutch of all narrowness.
Kabîr says: "I have attained the unattainable, and my heart is coloured with the colour of love."

XLIX

I. 105. *jo dîsai, so to hai nâhîn*

That which you see is not: and for that which is, you have no words.
Unless you see, you believe not: what is told you you cannot accept.
He who is discerning knows by the word; and the ignorant stands gaping.
Some contemplate the Formless, and others meditate on form:
but the wise man knows that Brahma is beyond both.
That beauty of His is not seen of the eye: that metre of His is not heard of the ear.
Kabîr says: "He who has found both love and renunciation never descends to death."

L

I. 126. *muralî bajat akhand sadâye*

The flute of the Infinite is played without ceasing, and its

sound is love:
When love renounces all limits, it reaches truth.
How widely the fragrance spreads! It has no end, nothing stands in its way.
The form of this melody is bright like a million suns:
incomparably sounds the vina, the vina of the notes of truth.

LI

I. 129. *sakhiyo, ham hûn bhâî vâlamâs'î*

Dear friend, I am eager to meet my Beloved! My youth has flowered, and the pain of separation from Him troubles my breast.
I am wandering yet in the alleys of knowledge without purpose,
but I have received His news in these alleys of knowledge.
I have a letter from my Beloved: in this letter is an unutterable message, and now my fear of death is done away.
Kabîr says: "O my loving friend! I have got for my gift the Deathless One."

LII

I. 130. *sâîn vin dard kareje hoy*

When I am parted from my Beloved, my heart is full of misery: I have no comfort in the day, I have no sleep in the night. To whom shall I tell my sorrow?
The night is dark; the hours slip by. Because my Lord is absent,
I start up and tremble with fear.
Kabîr says: "Listen, my friend! there is no other satisfaction,
save in the encounter with the Beloved."

LIII

I. 122. *kaum muralî s'abd s'un ânand bhayo*

What is that flute whose music thrills me with joy?
The flame burns without a lamp;
The lotus blossoms without a root;
Flowers bloom in clusters;
The moon-bird is devoted to the moon;
With all its heart the rain-bird longs for the shower of rain;
But upon whose love does the Lover concentrate His entire life?

LIV

I. 112. *s'untâ nahî dhun kî khabar*

Have you not heard the tune which the Unstruck Music is playing?
In the midst of the chamber the harp of joy is gently and
sweetly played; and where is the need of going without to hear it?

If you have not drunk of the nectar of that One Love, what boots it though you should purge yourself of all stains?
The Kazi is searching the words of the Koran, and instructing others: but if his heart be not steeped in that love, what does it avail, though he be a teacher of men?
The Yogi dyes his garments with red: but if he knows naught of that colour of love, what does it avail though his garments be tinted?
Kabîr says: "Whether I be in the temple or the balcony, in the camp or in the flower garden, I tell you truly that every moment my Lord is taking His delight in me."

LV

I. 73. *bhakti kâ mârag jhînâ re*

Subtle is the path of love!
Therein there is no asking and no not-asking,
There one loses one's self at His feet,
There one is immersed in the joy of the seeking: plunged in the deeps of love as the fish in the water.
The lover is never slow in offering his head for his Lord's service.
Kabîr declares the secret of this love.

LVI

I. 68. *bhâi kôî satguru sant kahâwaî*

He is the real Sadhu, who can reveal the form of the Formless to the vision of these eyes:
Who teaches the simple way of attaining Him, that is other than rites or ceremonies:
Who does not make you close the doors, and hold the breath, and renounce the world:
Who makes you perceive the Supreme Spirit wherever the mind attaches itself:
Who teaches you to be still in the midst of all your activities.
Ever immersed in bliss, having no fear in his mind, he keeps the spirit of union in the midst of all enjoyments.
The infinite dwelling of the Infinite Being is everywhere: in earth, water, sky, and air:
Firm as the thunderbolt, the seat of the seeker is established above the void.
He who is within is without: I see Him and none else.

LVII

I. 66. *sâdho, s'abd sâdhnâ kîjai*

Receive that Word from which the Universe springeth!
That word is the Guru; I have heard it, and become the disciple.

How many are there who know the meaning of that word?

O Sadhu! practise that Word!
The Vedas and the Puranas proclaim it,
The world is established in it,
The Rishis and devotees speak of it:
But none knows the mystery of the Word.
The householder leaves his house when he hears it,
The ascetic comes back to love when he hears it,
The Six Philosophies expound it,
The Spirit of Renunciation points to that Word,
From that Word the world-form has sprung,
That Word reveals all.
Kabîr says: "But who knows whence the Word cometh?

LVIII

I. 63. *pîle pyâlâ, ho matwâlâ*

Empty the Cup! O be drunken!
Drink the divine nectar of His Name!
Kabîr says: "Listen to me, dear Sadhu!
From the sole of the foot to the crown of the head this mind is filled with poison."

LIX

I. 52. *khasm na cînhai bâwari*

O man, if thou dost not know thine own Lord, whereof art thou so proud?
Put thy cleverness away: mere words shall never unite thee to Him.
Do not deceive thyself with the witness of the Scriptures:
Love is something other than this, and he who has sought it truly has found it.

LX

I. 56. *sukh sindh kî sair kâ*

The savour of wandering in the ocean of deathless life has rid me of all my asking:
As the tree is in the seed, so all diseases are in this asking.

LXI

I. 48. *sukh sâgar men âîke*

When at last you are come to the ocean of happiness, do not go back thirsty.
Wake, foolish man! for Death stalks you. Here is pure water before you; drink it at every breath.

Do not follow the mirage on foot, but thirst for the nectar;
Dhruva, Prahlad, and Shukadeva have drunk of it, and also Raidas has tasted it:
The saints are drunk with love, their thirst is for love.
Kabîr says: "Listen to me, brother! The nest of fear is broken.
Not for a moment have you come face to face with the world:
You are weaving your bondage of falsehood,
your words are full of deception:
With the load of desires which you. hold on your head, how can you be light?"
Kabîr says: "Keep within you truth, detachment, and love."

LXII

I. 35. *satî ko kaun s'ikhâwtâ hai*

Who has ever taught the widowed wife to burn herself on the pyre of her dead husband?
And who has ever taught love to find bliss in renunciation?

LXIII

I. 39. *are man, dhîraj kâhe na dharai*

Why so impatient, my heart?
He who watches over birds, beasts, and insects,
He who cared for you whilst you were yet in your mother's womb,
Shall He not care for you now that you are come forth?
Oh my heart, how could you turn from the smile of your Lord and wander so far from Him?
You have left Your Beloved and are thinking of others: and this is why all your work is in vain.

LXIV

I. 117. *sâîn se lagan kathin hai, bhâî*

Now hard it is to meet my Lord!
The rain-bird wails in thirst for the rain: almost she dies of her longing, yet she would have none other water than the rain.
Drawn by the love of music, the deer moves forward: she dies as she listens to the music, yet she shrinks not in fear.
The widowed wife sits by the body of her dead husband: she is not afraid of the fire.
Put away all fear for this poor body.

LXV

I. 22. *jab main bhûlâ, re bhâî*

O brother! when I was forgetful, my true Guru showed me the Way.

Then I left off all rites and ceremonies, I bathed no more in the holy water:
Then I learned that it was I alone who was mad, and the whole world beside me was sane; and I had disturbed these wise people.
From that time forth I knew no more how to roll in the dust in obeisance:
I do not ring the temple bell:
I do not set the idol on its throne:
I do not worship the image with flowers.
It is not the austerities that mortify the flesh which are pleasing to the Lord,
When you leave off your clothes and kill your senses, you do not please the Lord:
The man who is kind and who practises righteousness, who remains passive amidst the affairs of the world, who considers all creatures on earth as his own self,
He attains the Immortal Being, the true God is ever with him.
Kabîr says: "He attains the true Name whose words are pure, and who is free from pride and conceit."

LXVI

I. 20. *man na rangâye*

The Yogi dyes his garments, instead of dyeing his mind in the colours of love:
He sits within the temple of the Lord, leaving Brahma to worship a stone.
He pierces holes in his ears, he has a great beard and matted locks, he looks like a goat:
He goes forth into the wilderness, killing all his desires, and turns himself into an eunuch:
He shaves his head and dyes his garments; he reads the Gîtâ and becomes a mighty talker.
Kabîr says: "You are going to the doors of death, bound hand and foot!"

LXVII

I. 9. *nâ jâne sâhab kaisâ hai*

I do not know what manner of God is mine.
The Mullah cries aloud to Him: and why? Is your Lord deaf? The subtle anklets that ring on the feet of an insect when it moves are heard of Him.
Tell your beads, paint your forehead with the mark of your God, and wear matted locks long and showy: but a deadly weapon is in your heart, and how shall you have God?

LXVIII

III. 102. *ham se rahâ na jây*

I hear the melody of His flute, and I cannot contain myself:
The flower blooms, though it is not spring; and already the bee has received its invitation.
The sky roars and the lightning flashes, the waves arise in my heart,
The rain falls; and my heart longs for my Lord.
Where the rhythm of the world rises and falls, thither my heart has reached:
There the hidden banners are fluttering in the air.
Kabîr says: "My heart is dying, though it lives."

LXIX

III. 2. *jo khodâ masjid vasat hai*

If God be within the mosque, then to whom does this world belong?
If Ram be within the image which you find upon your pilgrimage, then who is there to know what happens without?
Hari is in the East: Allah is in the West. Look within your heart, for there you will find both Karim and Ram;
All the men and women of the world are His living forms.
Kabîr is the child of Allah and of Ram: He is my Guru, He is my Pir.

LXX

III. 9. *s'îl santosh sadâ samadrishti*

He who is meek and contented., he who has an equal vision, whose mind is filled with the fullness of acceptance and of rest;
He who has seen Him and touched Him, he is freed from all fear and trouble.
To him the perpetual thought of God is like sandal paste smeared on the body, to him nothing else is delight:
His work and his rest are filled with music: he sheds abroad the radiance of love.
Kabîr says: "Touch His feet, who is one and indivisible, immutable and peaceful; who fills all vessels to the brim with joy, and whose form is love."

LXXI

III. 13. *sâdh sangat pîtam*

Go thou to the company of the good, where the Beloved One has His dwelling place:
Take all thy thoughts and love and instruction from thence.
Let that assembly be burnt to ashes where His Name is not spoken!
Tell me, how couldst thou hold a wedding-feast, if the bridegroom himself were not there?
Waver no more, think only of the Beloved;

Set not thy heart on the worship of other gods, there is no worth in the worship of other masters.
Kabîr deliberates and says: "Thus thou shalt never find the Beloved!"

LXXII

III. 26. *tor hîrâ hirâilwâ kîcad men*

The jewel is lost in the mud, and all are seeking for it;
Some look for it in the east, and some in the west; some in the water and some amongst stones.
But the servant Kabîr has appraised it at its true value, and has wrapped it with care in the end of the mantle of his heart.

LXXIII

III. 26. *âyau din gaune kâ ho*

The palanquin came to take me away to my husband's home, and it sent through my heart a thrill of joy;
But the bearers have brought me into the lonely forest, where I have no one of my own.
O bearers, I entreat you by your feet, wait but a moment longer:
let me go back to my kinsmen and friends, and take my leave of them.
The servant Kabîr sings: "O Sadhu! finish your buying and selling, have done with your good and your bad: for there are no markets and no shops in the land to which you go."

LXXIV

III. 30. *are dil, prem nagar kä ant na pâyâ*

O my heart! you have not known all the secrets of this city of love: in ignorance you came, and in ignorance you return.
O my friend, what have you done with this life? You have taken on your head the burden heavy with stones, and who is to lighten it for you?
Your Friend stands on the other shore, but you never think in your mind how you may meet with Him:
The boat is broken, and yet you sit ever upon the bank; and thus you are beaten to no purpose by the waves.
The servant Kabîr asks you to consider; who is there that shall befriend you at the last?
You are alone, you have no companion: you will suffer the consequences of your own deeds.

LXXV

III. 55. *ved kahe sargun ke âge*

The Vedas say that the Unconditioned stands beyond
the world of Conditions.
O woman, what does it avail thee to dispute whether
He is beyond all or in all?
See thou everything as thine own dwelling place: the mist of
pleasure and pain can never spread there.
There Brahma is revealed day and night: there light is His
garment, light is His seat, light rests on thy head.
Kabîr says: "The Master, who is true, He is all light."

LXXVI

III. 48. *tû surat nain nihâr*

Open your eyes of love, and see Him who pervades this world I
consider it well, and know that this is your own country.
When you meet the true Guru, He will awaken your heart;
He will tell you the secret of love and detachment, and then you
will know indeed that He transcends this universe.
This world is the City of Truth, its maze of paths enchants the heart:
We can reach the goal without crossing the road, such is the sport unending.
Where the ring of manifold joys ever dances about Him, there is
the sport of Eternal Bliss.
When we know this, then all our receiving and renouncing is over;
Thenceforth the heat of having shall never scorch us more.

He is the Ultimate Rest unbounded:
He has spread His form of love throughout all the world.
From that Ray which is Truth, streams of new forms are
perpetually springing: and He pervades those forms.
All the gardens and groves and bowers are abounding with blossom;
and the air breaks forth into ripples of joy.
There the swan plays a wonderful game,
There the Unstruck Music eddies around the Infinite One;
There in the midst the Throne of the Unheld is shining, whereon
the great Being sits—
Millions of suns are shamed by the radiance of a single hair of His body.
On the harp of the road what true melodies are being sounded!
and its notes pierce the heart:
There the Eternal Fountain is playing its endless life-streams of
birth and death.
They call Him Emptiness who is the Truth of truths, in Whom all
truths are stored!

There within Him creation goes forward, which is beyond all
philosophy; for philosophy cannot attain to Him:
There is an endless world, O my Brother! and there is the
Nameless Being, of whom naught can be said.
Only he knows it who has reached that region: it is other than

all that is heard and said.
No form, no body, no length, no breadth is seen there: how can I tell you that which it is?
He comes to the Path of the Infinite on whom the grace of the Lord descends: he is freed from births and deaths who attains to Him.
Kabîr says: "It cannot be told by the words of the mouth, it cannot be written on paper:
It is like a dumb person who tastes a sweet thing—how shall it be explained?"

LXXVII

III. 60. *cal hamsâ wâ des' jahân1*

O my heart! let us go to that country where dwells the Beloved, the ravisher of my heart!
There Love is filling her pitcher from the well, yet she has no rope wherewith to draw water;
There the clouds do not cover the sky, yet the rain falls down in gentle showers:
O bodiless one! do not sit on your doorstep; go forth and bathe yourself in that rain!
There it is ever moonlight and never dark; and who speaks of one sun only? that land is illuminate with the rays of a million suns.

LXXVIII

III. 63. *kahain Kabîr, s'uno ho sâdho*

Kabîr says: "O Sadhu! hear my deathless words. If you want your own good, examine and consider them well.
You have estranged yourself from the Creator, of whom you have sprung: you have lost your reason, you have bought death.
All doctrines and all teachings are sprung from Him, from Him they grow: know this for certain, and have no fear.
Hear from me the tidings of this great truth!
Whose name do you sing, and on whom do you meditate? O, come forth from this entanglement!
He dwells at the heart of all things, so why take refuge in empty desolation?
If you place the Guru at a distance from you, then it is but the distance that you honour:
If indeed the Master be far away, then who is it else that is creating this world?
When you think that He is not here, then you wander further and further away, and seek Him in vain with tears.
Where He is far off, there He is unattainable: where He is near, He is very bliss.

Kabîr says: "Lest His servant should suffer pain He pervades him
through and through."
Know yourself then, O Kabîr; for He is in you from head to foot.
Sing with gladness, and keep your seat unmoved within your heart.

LXXIX

III. 66. *nâ main dharmî nahîn adharmî*

I am neither pious nor ungodly, I live neither by law nor by sense,
I am neither a speaker nor hearer, I am neither a servant nor
master, I am neither bond nor free,
I am neither detached nor attached.
I am far from none: I am near to none.
I shall go neither to hell nor to heaven.
I do all works; yet I am apart from all works.
Few comprehend my meaning: he who can comprehend it, he sits unmoved.
Kabîr seeks neither to establish nor to destroy.

LXXX

III. 69. *satta nâm hai sab ten nyârâ*

The true Name is like none other name!
The distinction of the Conditioned from the Unconditioned is but a word:
The Unconditioned is the seed, the Conditioned is the flower and the fruit.
Knowledge is the branch, and the Name is the root.
Look, and see where the root is: happiness shall be yours when
you come to the root.
The root will lead you to the branch, the leaf, the flower, and the fruit:
It is the encounter with the Lord, it is the attainment of bliss,
it is the reconciliation of the Conditioned and the Unconditioned.

LXXXI

III. 74. *pratham ek jo âpai âp*

In the beginning was He alone, sufficient unto Himself: the
formless, colourless, and unconditioned Being.
Then was there neither beginning, middle, nor end;
Then were no eyes, no darkness, no light;
Then were no ground, air, nor sky; no fire, water, nor earth; no
rivers like the Ganges and the Jumna, no seas, oceans, and waves.
Then was neither vice nor virtue; scriptures there were not, as
the Vedas and Puranas, nor as the Koran.
Kabîr ponders in his mind and says, "Then was there no activity:
the Supreme Being remained merged in the unknown depths of
His own self."
The Guru neither eats nor drinks, neither lives nor dies:
Neither has He form, line, colour, nor vesture.

He who has neither caste nor clan nor anything else—how may I describe His glory?
He has neither form nor formlessness,
He has no name,
He has neither colour nor colourlessness,
He has no dwelling-place.

LXXXII

III. 76. *kahain Kabîr vicâr ke*

Kabîr ponders and says: "He who has neither caste nor country, who is formless and without quality, fills all space."
The Creator brought into being the Game of Joy: and from the word Om the Creation sprang.
The earth is His joy; His joy is the sky;
His joy is the flashing of the sun and the moon;
His joy is the beginning, the middle, and the end;
His joy is eyes, darkness, and light.
Oceans and waves are His joy: His joy the Sarasvati, the Jumna, and the Ganges.
The Guru is One: and life and death., union and separation, are all His plays of joy!
His play the land and water, the whole universe!
His play the earth and the sky!
In play is the Creation spread out, in play it is established.
The whole world, says Kabîr, rests in His play, yet still the Player remains unknown.

LXXXIII

III. 84. *jhî jhî jantar bâjai*

The harp gives forth murmurous music; and the dance goes on without hands and feet.
It is played without fingers, it is heard without ears: for He is the ear, and He is the listener.
The gate is locked, but within there is fragrance: and there the meeting is seen of none.
The wise shall understand it.

LXXXIV

III. 89. *mor phakîrwâ mângi jây*

The Beggar goes a-begging, but
I could not even catch sight of Him:
And what shall I beg of the Beggar He gives without my asking.
Kabîr says: "I am His own: now let that befall which may befall!"

LXXXV

III. 90. *naihar se jiyarâ phât re*

My heart cries aloud for the house of my lover; the open road and
the shelter of a roof are all one to her who has lost the city of her husband.
My heart finds no joy in anything: my mind and my body are distraught.
His palace has a million gates, but there is a vast ocean between it and me:
How shall I cross it, O friend? for endless is the outstretching of the path.
How wondrously this lyre is wrought! When its strings are
rightly strung, it maddens the heart: but when the keys are
broken and the strings are loosened, none regard it more.
I tell my parents with laughter that I must go to my Lord in the morning;

They are angry, for they do not want me to go, and they say:
"She thinks she has gained such dominion over her husband that she
can have whatsoever she wishes; and therefore she is impatient to go to
him."
Dear friend, lift my veil lightly now; for this is the night of love.
Kabîr says: "Listen to me! My heart is eager to meet my lover:
I lie sleepless upon my bed. Remember me early in the morning!"

LXXXVI

III. 96. *jîv mahal men S'iv pahunwâ*

Serve your God, who has come into this temple of life!
Do not act the part of a madman, for the night is thickening fast.
He has awaited me for countless ages, for love of me He has lost His heart:
Yet I did not know the bliss that was so near to me, for my love
was not yet awake.
But now, my Lover has made known to me the meaning of the note
that struck my ear:
Now, my good fortune is come.
Kabîr says: "Behold! how great is my good fortune! I have
received the unending caress of my Beloved!"

LXXXVII

I. 71. *gagan ghatâ ghaharânî, sâdho*

Clouds thicken in the sky! O, listen to the deep voice of their roaring;
The rain comes from the east with its monotonous murmur.
Take care of the fences and boundaries of your fields, lest the
rains overflow them;
Prepare the soil of deliverance, and let the creepers of love and
renunciation be soaked in this shower.
It is the prudent farmer who will bring his harvest home; he
shall fill both his vessels, and feed both the wise men and the saints.

LXXXVIII

III. 118. *âj din ke main jaun balihârî*

This day is dear to me above all other days, for to-day the Beloved Lord is a guest in my house;
My chamber and my courtyard are beautiful with His presence.
My longings sing His Name, and they are become lost in His great beauty:
I wash His feet, and I look upon His Face; and I lay before Him as an offering my body, my mind, and all that I have.
What a day of gladness is that day in which my Beloved, who is my treasure, comes to my house!
All evils fly from my heart when I see my Lord.
"My love has touched Him; my heart is longing for the Name which is Truth."
Thus sings Kabîr, the servant of all servants.

LXXXIX

I. 100. *kôi s'untâ hai jñânî râg gagan men*

Is there any wise man who will listen to that solemn music which arises in the sky?
For He, the Source of all music, makes all vessels full fraught, and rests in fullness Himself.
He who is in the body is ever athirst, for he pursues that which is in part:
But ever there wells forth deeper and deeper the sound "He is this—this is He"; fusing love and renunciation into one.
Kabîr says: "O brother! that is the Primal Word."

XC

I. 108. *main kâ se bûjhaun*

To whom shall I go to learn about my Beloved?
Kabîr says: "As you never may find the forest if you ignore the tree, so He may never be found in abstractions."

XCI

III. 12. *samskirit bhâshâ padhi lînhâ*

I have learned the Sanskrit language, so let all men call me wise:
But where is the use of this, when I am floating adrift, and parched with thirst, and burning with the heat of desire?
To no purpose do you bear on your head this load of pride and vanity.
Kabîr says: "Lay it down in the dust, and go forth to meet the Beloved. Address Him as your Lord."

XCII

III. 110. *carkhâ calai surat virahin kâ*

The woman who is parted from her lover spins at the spinning wheel.
The city of the body arises in its beauty; and within it the palace of the mind has been built.
The wheel of love revolves in the sky, and the seat is made of the jewels of knowledge:
What subtle threads the woman weaves, and makes them fine with love and reverence!
Kabîr says: "I am weaving the garland of day and night. When my Lover comes and touches me with His feet, I shall offer Him my tears."

XCIII

III. 111. *kotîn bhânu candra târâgan*

Beneath the great umbrella of my King millions of suns and moons and stars are shining!
He is the Mind within my mind: He is the Eye within mine eye.
Ah, could my mind and eyes be one! Could my love but reach to my Lover! Could but the fiery heat of my heart be cooled!
Kabîr says: "When you unite love with the Lover, then you have love's perfection."

XCIV

I. 92. *avadhû begam des' hamârâ*

O sadhu! my land is a sorrowless land.
I cry aloud to all, to the king and the beggar, the emperor and the fakir—
Whosoever seeks for shelter in the Highest, let all come and settle in my land!
Let the weary come and lay his burdens here!

So live here, my brother, that you may cross with ease to that other shore.
It is a land without earth or sky, without moon or stars;
For only the radiance of Truth shines in my Lord's Durbar.
Kabîr says: "O beloved brother! naught is essential save Truth."

XCV

I. 109. *sâîn ke sangat sâsur âî*

Came with my Lord to my Lord's home: but I lived not with Him and I tasted Him not, and my youth passed away like a dream.
On my wedding night my women-friends sang in chorus, and I was anointed with the unguents of pleasure and pain:
But when the ceremony was over, I left my Lord and came away, and my kinsman tried to console me upon the road.

Kabîr says, "I shall go to my Lord's house with my love at my side; then shall I sound the trumpet of triumph!"

XCVI

I. 75. *samajh dekh man mît piyarwâ*

O friend, dear heart of mine, think well! if you love indeed, then why do you sleep?
If you have found Him, then give yourself utterly, and take Him to you.
Why do you loose Him again and again?
If the deep sleep of rest has come to your eyes, why waste your time making the bed and arranging the pillows?
Kabîr says: "I tell you the ways of love! Even though the head itself must be given, why should you weep over it?"

XCVII

II. 90. *sâhab ham men, sâhab tum men*

The Lord is in me, the Lord is in you, as life is in every seed.
O servant! put false pride away, and seek for Him within you.
A million suns are ablaze with light,
The sea of blue spreads in the sky,
The fever of life is stilled, and all stains are washed away;
when I sit in the midst of that world.
Hark to the unstruck bells and drums! Take your delight in love!
Rains pour down without water, and the rivers are streams of light.
One Love it is that pervades the whole world, few there are who know it fully:
They are blind who hope to see it by the light of reason, that reason which is the cause of separation—
The House of Reason is very far away!
How blessed is Kabîr, that amidst this great joy he sings within his own vessel.
It is the music of the meeting of soul with soul;
It is the music of the forgetting of sorrows;
It is the music that transcends all coming in and all going forth.

XCVIII

II. 98. *ritu phâgun niyarânî*

The month of March draws near: ah, who will unite me to my Lover?
How shall I find words for the beauty of my Beloved? For He is merged in all beauty.
His colour is in all the pictures of the world, and it bewitches the body and the mind.
Those who know this, know what is this unutterable play of the Spring.
Kabîr says: "Listen to me, brother' there are not many who have

found this out."

XCIX

II. 111. *Nârad, pyâr so antar nâhî*

Oh Narad! I know that my Lover cannot be far:
When my Lover wakes, I wake; when He sleeps, I sleep.
He is destroyed at the root who gives pain to my Beloved.
Where they sing His praise, there I live;
When He moves, I walk before Him: my heart yearns for my Beloved.
The infinite pilgrimage lies at His feet, a million devotees are seated there.
Kabîr says: "The Lover Himself reveals the glory of true love."

C

II. 122. *kôî prem kî peng jhulâo re*

Hang up the swing of love to-day! Hang the body and the mind between the arms of the Beloved, in the ecstasy of love's joy:
Bring the tearful streams of the rainy clouds to your eyes, and cover your heart with the shadow of darkness:
Bring your face nearer to His ear, and speak of the deepest longings of your heart.
Kabîr says: "Listen to me, brother! bring the vision of the Beloved in your heart."

Lector House believes that a society develops through a two-fold approach of continuous learning and adaptation, which is derived from the study of classic literary works spread across the historic timeline of literature records. Therefore, we aim at reviving, repairing and redeveloping all those inaccessible or damaged but historically as well as culturally important literature across subjects so that the future generations may have an opportunity to study and learn from past works to embark upon a journey of creating a better future.

This book is a result of an effort made by Lector House towards making a contribution to the preservation and repair of original ancient works which might hold historical significance to the approach of continuous learning across subjects.

HAPPY READING & LEARNING!

LECTOR HOUSE LLP
E-MAIL: lectorpublishing@gmail.com

9 789389 956924